Ken Griffey, Sr., and Ken Griffey, Jr.

Father and Son Teammates

by Bill Gutman

MILLBROOK SPORTS WORLD

THE MILLBROOK PRESS

BROOKFIELD, CONNECTICUT

Published by The Millbrook Press
2 Old New Milford Road
Brookfield, CT 06804

Created in association with Grey Castle Press, Inc.
Series Editorial Director: *Elizabeth Simon*
Art Director: *Nancy Driscoll*
Design Management: *Italiano-Perla Design*

Photographs courtesy of: Seattle Mariners: cover, 3; AP/Wide World
Photos: 4, 8, 10-11, 15, 16, 27, 30-31, 33, 36, 43, 44; Cincinnati Reds: 12;
The Cincinnati Enquirer: 14, 18, 20; *The Bellingham Herald:* 22;
The Seattle Times: 40, 46.

Library of Congress Cataloging-in-Publication Data

Gutman, Bill.
Ken Griffey, Sr., and Ken Griffey, Jr.: father and son teammates / by Bill Gutman
p. cm — (Millbrook sports world)
Includes bibliographical references (p. 46) and index.
Summary: a biography of the father and son whose professional baseball careers
came together when they both played for the Seattle Mariners.
ISBN 0–395–66816–6 (pbk.)
1. Griffey, Ken —Juvenile literature.
2. Griffey, Ken. 1950- —Juvenile literature.
3. Baseball players—United States—Biography—Juvenile literature.
4. Seattle Mariners (Baseball team)—History—Juvenile liter.
[1. Griffey, Ken. 2. Griffey, Ken. 1950- . 3. Baseball players.
4. Afro-Americans—Biography.] I. Title. II. Series.
GV865.G69G88 1993
796.357'092'2—dc20
[B]
92-18162   CIP AC

Printed in the United States of America
123456789-WO-96 95 94 93 92

KEN GRIFFEY, SR., AND KEN GRIFFEY, JR.

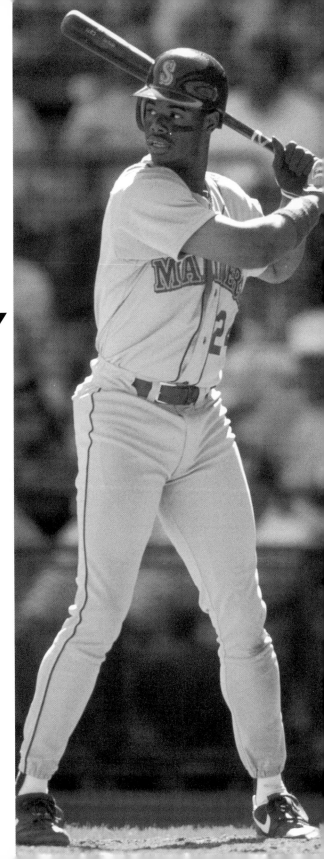

Ken Griffey, Sr., felt a rush of nerves as he trotted out to left field. Griffey was 40 years old and was playing his 18th season of big-league baseball. He had been a star with the fabled Cincinnati Reds teams of the mid-1970s. They were known as the "Big Red Machine" and already had won a pair of World Series.

Yet on the night of August 31, 1990, this long-time ball player was nervous. He was with the Seattle Mariners now, and this was his first game with his new team. He looked up at the crowd of 27,166 fans at the Kingdome. He knew they would be rooting for him as the newest member of the Mariners.

It took a couple of innings before the ball player finally shook the jitters. The Kansas City Royals' Bo Jackson was up at bat. This was before

Baseball history was about to be made when the Seattle
Mariners signed Ken Griffey, Sr., on August 30, 1990.

his severe hip injury in 1990, and he could really fly around the bases. Jackson hit a shot down the left field line and took off. Griffey raced toward the bullpen. He grabbed the ball on a carom off the wall. Then he whirled and fired hard toward second base. Second baseman Harold Reynolds grabbed the strong throw, turned, and tagged Jackson out. The Seattle crowd roared.

The first thing Griffey did after making an outstanding play was look toward center field. There he saw the Mariners' center fielder, Ken Griffey, Jr., grinning from ear to ear.

"It runs in the family," Griffey, Jr., shouted from his position in center.

The elder Griffey smiled. He had dreamed of the day he would play alongside his son in the same big-league outfield. A father and son had never before played in the big leagues at the same time—let alone on the same team. The Griffeys were the first. After the game, Ken Griffey, Sr., would tell everyone how exciting it was for him.

"You can talk about the 1976 batting race, the two World Series I played in, and the All-Star games," he said, "but this is number one. This is the best thing that's ever happened to me. This is the pinnacle."

Ken, Jr., his 20-year-old son and already considered a future superstar, seemed to make light of the moment. "It seemed like a father-son game," he said, "like we were out in the backyard playing catch."

But it was, indeed, a very special occasion. When Ken Griffey, Jr., became the Seattle Mariners' center fielder in 1989, his father was playing for Cincinnati. The two made history then. They were the first father and son to play in the major leagues at the same time. When Cincinnati released

Griffey, Sr., in August of 1990, the Mariners quickly signed him. That's what led to the August 31 game with Kansas City. Both Griffeys were now on the same team and could play together in the same outfield.

Even Bo Jackson, the victim of that great fielding play and throw by Griffey, Sr., knew it was a special moment. "I didn't expect a perfect bounce and to have that old guy throw me out," Jackson said. "I'd have been mad if anyone else had thrown me out, but it was a piece of history."

Bo Jackson was right. It was a piece of history, one that had the entire baseball world watching.

GRIFFEY, SR., SETS THE STAGE

In baseball, many sons have followed their fathers into the big leagues. But because Ken Griffey, Sr., and Ken Griffey, Jr., made baseball history together, their stories will always be linked—just as their baseball careers have been.

George Kenneth Griffey, Sr., was born in Donora, Pennsylvania, on April 10, 1950. Donora was already known as a town that had produced a great ballplayer. Hall of Fame star Stan "The Man" Musial came out of Donora and went on to an incredible career with the St. Louis Cardinals. Musial starred with the Cards during the 1950s while Griffey, Sr., was growing up.

There is another connection. Buddy Griffey, Ken's father, was a high school teammate of Stan the Man. Musial remembers Buddy as a left-handed throwing third baseman and also as a football star at Donora High. Good athletic ability ran in the Griffey family.

But Ken, Sr., didn't have an easy time growing up. His father left the family when Ken was only two years old. His mother, Ruth Griffey, had to raise her six children by working odd jobs and sometimes had to rely on welfare checks. Buddy Griffey returned some seven years later, and Ken didn't know him. The two have never really been close.

None of that stopped Ken, Sr., from becoming a fine all-around athlete. At Donora High, he was a football, track, and baseball star. At the time, he was known more for football and track than for baseball. Yet the Cincinnati Reds thought he had great natural ability and picked him on the 29th round of the 1969 draft.

Griffey, Sr., was married by that time, and his wife, Alberta, was expecting a child. It couldn't have been easy for them. He was playing in the low minors, and still didn't know whether or not he would make it to the majors.

Griffey, Sr., spent four years working his way through the minors. In 1973 he came up to the Reds and played in 25 games. A year later he played in 88 games, and by 1975 was the regular right fielder on the best team of the decade.

The Reds won the World Series in 1975 and 1976 and became known as the Big Red Machine for their great hitting. The team was loaded with stars. Griffey, Sr., played alongside such players as Pete Rose, Joe Morgan, Johnny Bench, Tony Perez, George Foster, Dave Concepcion, and Cesar Geronimo. Griffey quickly became a top hitter. He batted .305

Ken Griffey, Sr., hit his peak during his years with the Cincinnati Reds.

in 1975 and .336 in 1976. By age 26 he was considered one of the finer young players in the National League.

Ken Griffey, Sr., was 5 feet 11 (180 centimeters) and weighed 190 pounds (86 kilograms). He was a good runner and stole 34 bases in 1976. He didn't hit a lot of home runs, but he always got his share of doubles and triples. He was also a fine defensive outfielder, and was considered an excellent all-around ball player. He had settled in for a long career.

FOLLOWING IN THE FOOTSTEPS

On November 21, 1969, George Kenneth Griffey, Jr., was born, and two years later a second son, Craig, was born. Griffey, Sr., and his wife Alberta tried to keep the

Griffey, Sr., slams a game-winning double to left center off Red Sox pitcher Dick Drago in the ninth inning of the second game of the 1975 World Series. The Boston Red Sox catcher is Carlton Fisk.

family together as much as possible. As a result, Griffey, Sr., developed a closeness with his sons during his four years in the minors.

"I was always with them and had them with me much of the time," he said.

Because he grew up around baseball, Ken, Jr., decided at a young age to follow in his father's footsteps. However, it isn't always easy to do this. To try to equal the success of a famous parent can sometimes put pressure on a child as he or she grows up.

But young Ken learned early about being a professional ball player. He also developed an understanding for the game before most boys.

One day, when his father was playing winter ball in Puerto Rico, Ken, Jr., who was just six years old, was watching from the dugout. When Griffey, Sr., struck out, young Ken said, "That pitcher's got nothing," trying to encourage his father. But when he came up a second time, Griffey, Sr., struck out again. This time his son piped up, "Dad, *you* got nothing."

Everyone laughed. If nothing else, young Ken already had a feel for the game. Pretty soon he would be getting a real taste of what the big leagues were like. It wasn't long before his father took him to Riverfront Stadium in Cincinnati. Ken, Jr., often spent time in the dugout and in the locker room. He met all the big stars on the Reds and some players from other teams as well. It was the kind of thing many young boys dream about.

The Griffeys gathered at Riverfront Stadium in Cincinnati
for family days and other special events. Here, Ken, Sr., has
his arms around younger son, Craig, while Ken, Jr., looks on.
The boys' mother, Alberta, stands behind them.

He also met the sons of other Big Red Machine players. At one time or another he played ball with Pete Rose, Jr., Eduardo and Victor Perez, Lee May, Jr., and Brian McRae. Someone dubbed the group the "Little Red Machine."

"They were wild, and you had to keep after them," said Tony Perez, who played both third and first base for Cincinnati. "But they were good kids."

Ken, Jr., soon began playing in Little League. He was an outstanding player right from the beginning. Oddly, he didn't think of his father as a baseball star back then. He says his most vivid memory from those early days was the 1980 All-Star Game.

"That's the one time Dad impressed me," Ken, Jr., said. "He hit a home run and was named the Most Valuable Player of the game. But mostly it didn't matter what he did on the field. He was just Dad."

Life changed for the Griffey family after the 1981 season. That's when

At the age of eight, Ken, Jr., was a star pitcher and outfielder for the Mt. Airy D-1 team in Cincinnati.

Griffey, Sr., was traded to the New York Yankees for a pair of minor lea-guers. He had hit .311 in the strike-shortened season of 1981. But the entire team was aging and had to be rebuilt. Some thought the club didn't want to pay Griffey a star's salary any longer.

The Yankees still had a solid team in 1982. It was the team that had starred Babe Ruth, Lou Gehrig, Joe DiMaggio, and Mickey Mantle over the years. But for Griffey, Sr., going to the Yankees meant having to leave his family in Cincinnati.

Ken, Sr., receives the Most Valuable Player trophy for his performance in the National League in the 1980 All-Star Game at Los Angeles. Presenting the award is then Commissioner of Baseball Bowie Kuhn.

His Yankee years weren't happy ones. He often found himself pla-tooned. That meant he didn't play in all the games. He hit .306 in 1983, but batted in the .270s his three other full seasons with the Yanks. By 1986, when he was traded to the Atlanta Braves, Griffey, Sr., was 36 years old. A player who is that old is usually get-ting close to retirement. Griffey, Sr., didn't know how much longer he would play.

While Griffey, Sr., was away play-ing for the Yanks, young Ken was growing up. He was getting taller and stronger and was becoming a better

Griffey, Sr., was traded to the New York Yankees for the 1982 season.
Here he is introduced to the New York media by Yankee first-baseman
Bob Watson, as Alberta Griffey looks on.

baseball player each year. Because the family remained in Cincinnati, and Ken, Sr., was playing in New York, father and son didn't see much of each other during the baseball season.

"If I needed to talk to him, I would call him after the game," said Ken, Jr. "If I did something wrong [on the field] Dad would sometimes fly me to New York and tell me what I should have done. Then he would send me home the next day, and I'd play baseball."

Not many young players had a personal coach who would fly him part way across the country to give him some tips. The tips and young Ken's ability were beginning to be noticed. By the time he was 14, Ken, Jr., was attracting pro scouts. He already looked like a future major leaguer.

NUMBER ONE PICK

When her son was 16 years old, Alberta Griffey felt he had outgrown Little League and was good enough to play Connie Mack League baseball. The Connie Mack League is an amateur league with teams all around the country. It is much like Little League or Babe Ruth League, but for older kids. It is named after Hall of Fame star Connie Mack, who managed the Philadelphia Athletics for fifty years.

Because Griffey, Sr., was away so much, he wasn't sure it was a good idea. Mrs. Griffey said it took her nearly three months to convince her husband that Junior, as he was called, was good enough. Finally, Griffey, Sr., agreed, and Junior went on to lead his team to the Connie Mack World Series. In the series he hit three homers. One was to left field, one to center, and the other to right. It seemed as if Mrs. Griffey was going to be her son's best scout.

Ken, Jr., was also starring for Moeller High School in Cincinnati at this time. Moeller has long been known nationally as a high school football power. Being an outstanding athlete, young Ken was also a fine football player. He was tall, strong, and very fast. It was no surprise that he became a fine tailback for the Moeller gridders. He was also the star of the baseball team.

Junior was so good that he played varsity football as well as varsity baseball right from his freshman year. During this time, Griffey, Sr., was

playing in New York, then Atlanta. So he rarely saw his son play high school baseball. Football was different, however. That was played in the fall after the baseball season was over. Griffey, Sr., would return home and watch Junior run out of the tailback position. He felt that his son might even have a future in football.

But all that changed in the fall of 1986 when Junior started his senior year at Moeller. He made his own decision to give up football and concentrate on his final baseball season. There was little doubt now what he wanted to do. But Griffey, Sr., wasn't sure at first that his son had made the right move.

As a split-end and tailback on the Moeller High School football team in Cincinnati, Junior was so outstanding that even his father thought he had a future in the sport.

"It was his [Ken, Jr.'s,] decision," said Griffey, Sr. "I wanted to see him play football, but he had all these baseball scouts watching him, and all he talked about was playing baseball."

Junior was a power-hitting outfielder for Moeller. He was good enough to be named the Player of the Year in the conference after both his junior and senior years. He was already taller than his father, standing 6 feet 3 (191 centimeters) and weighing 195 pounds (88 kilograms). Like his father, Ken, Jr., was a left-handed batter. But he was more of a power hitter than his father. The younger Griffey had a full stroke that could send the ball a long way.

The only thing that seemed to bother Ken, Jr., on a baseball field was knowing that his father was in the stands. His coach at Moeller High, Mike Cameron, remembers these times.

"Only when his father was there would Kenny pressure himself," Coach Cameron recalled. "A hundred scouts could be in the stands, and it wouldn't make a difference."

Even Ken, Jr., admitted that for a period of a few years he tried too hard when his father was watching. "When he [Griffey, Sr.] was there, it was the only time I thought I had to impress somebody," he said. "But he'd tell me he was the one guy I *didn't* have to impress."

Yet until he hit a single in the late fall of 1987, Junior had not gotten a base hit in front of his father since 1982. Perhaps it was the pressure of following in the footsteps of a famous father.

Otherwise, things couldn't have been better. Junior had an outstanding senior year with Moeller. Then, just before his graduation in June, he heard

the news he had been waiting for. The Seattle Mariners had made him the nation's number one pick in the 1987 amateur draft. At the age of 17, Ken Griffey, Jr., was about to become a professional baseball player.

MINOR LEAGUES, MAJOR CRISIS

Ken Griffey, Jr., had no doubts about signing with the Mariners. His first contract called for a bonus of between $150,000 and $160,000. Seattle had never had a winning season or been in a pennant race. Nor had Griffey, Sr., been offered a bonus when he signed with Cincinnati back in 1969. Junior was more than happy to sign.

"My son considers himself a winner," said Griffey, Sr., "He feels that one day he can help turn the franchise around."

Ken, Jr., was drafted by Seattle on June 2, 1987. He graduated from Moeller a few days later, signed his contract with the Mariners, and found himself headed for Bellingham, Washington. Bellingham was in the Northwest League, a good starting point for young ball players. The Northwest League played a short season. It was just enough for teenagers to get a feel for professional baseball and for the club to take a look at its young prospects.

But there can be more to it than that. Young men like Ken Griffey, Jr., are often going far away from home for the first time. This wasn't easy for Ken. Bellingham was about 90 miles (145 kilometers) north of Seattle,

Junior was the best player on the Moeller High baseball team. This picture was taken in May 1987, about a month before he became the top draft choice of the American League Seattle Mariners.

Washington (home of the Mariners) and just 20 miles (32 kilometers) from the Canadian border. It was a different kind of place for Ken. For one thing, there were very few black people.

"Things are a little different here," young Griffey said. "It will take some getting used to for me. But I have to mature. That's why I'm here."

At first it seemed that he was handling things well. His play on the field quickly showed why he was such a bright prospect. His first hit as a pro

At Bellingham, Washington, in the Northwest League, Griffey, Jr., showed his big-league potential as a 17 year old.

came on June 17 when he slammed a home run against Everett. This was barely more than two weeks after he graduated from high school. Things were happening fast. During the rest of the week young Griffey hit 3 homers, drove in 8 runs, and stole 4 bases. For his efforts he was named Northwest League Player of the Week.

But he still had to improve his concentration. Twice in the early going he was picked off first because he was daydreaming. "He's got to learn to stay ahead mentally," said his manager, Rick Sweet. "You can't be a spectator when you're out there playing the game."

There were things to get used to off the field as well. For example, the team traveled in an old, 1958 school bus. It didn't have a bathroom, and some of the trips were ten hours long.

"[The conditions were] a whole lot worse than I ever imagined," he would admit later.

Homesickness was another problem. Young Griffey missed his family and friends. The phone bills to Cincinnati were huge, but calling home was his only link to his loved ones. More than once he thought he wasn't ready, that maybe he should pack up and go back to Cincinnati. But his mother and his girlfriend back home made him believe he should stick it out.

What people didn't know then was that there were other pressures building up. The team bus driver had two teen-aged sons, and young Griffey said later that one of them called him a "nigger," and the other threatened to come after him with a gun. For a young player trying to adjust to professional baseball, dealing with this kind of racism and the threat of violence had to be very upsetting.

Then on July 4, Ken, Jr., was injured crashing into the center-field wall. He was a speedy and daring outfielder and had never hesitated to go after the ball to try to make a great catch. He hurt his shoulder and had to sit out a week. When he came back on July 12, he caught fire. From that day until August 13, he ripped away, batting .453 with another 7 homers and 16 runs batted in (RBIs).

When the Bellingham season ended, Ken, Jr., had a solid .320 average and led the team with 14 homers, 40 RBIs, and 13 stolen bases. He was named to the all-league team and also voted the top major-league prospect in the Northwest League by *Baseball America*. Despite some difficult adjustments, it looked like a very successful first year.

But young Griffey still couldn't go home to relax. The team wanted him to spend some time in the Instructional League in Arizona. So it was on to another strange place where he was coached on the fundamentals of the game. He finally returned home in the fall.

Ken, Jr.'s, homecoming didn't go smoothly. He hadn't had an easy time adjusting to professional baseball. First, having suffered racial prejudice put him on edge. Then there were times when some of his coaches yelled at him. This is not uncommon in sports, but it was something young Griffey wasn't used to.

Also, when he came home, Junior began to have problems with his father. "Dad wanted me to pay rent or get my own place," Ken, Jr., said. "I was confused and hurting. It seemed like everyone was yelling at me in baseball. Then when I came home everyone was yelling at me there. I got depressed. I got angry. I didn't want to live."

One day in January 1988, Griffey, Jr., was with his girlfriend and her brother. He was still depressed. He grabbed a big bottle of aspirin and swallowed its contents. His friends tried to stop him, but couldn't. A friend's mother drove him to Providence Hospital in Mount Airy, Ohio. Once there, his stomach was pumped, and he was put in the intensive care unit.

A scared and angry Griffey, Sr., rushed to the hospital and promptly got into another argument with his son.

"I ripped the IV [intravenous tube] out of my arm," said Griffey, Jr. "That stopped him yelling."

It was a crisis for the entire Griffey family and a story that didn't come out until early in 1992, when both father and son agreed to talk about it.

The story surprised everyone. On the outside, Griffey, Jr., seemed to take to pro ball with ease. His numbers proved that. But when a young person says he or she doesn't want to live, it's usually a cry for help.

The crisis marked the beginning of a different kind of relationship between father and son. Griffey, Jr., said he "wanted to cause some hurt for others" because he was hurting. He soon learned that he was only harming himself. Perhaps unwisely, neither Griffey sought any counseling after the incident. But they had many long, heart-to-heart talks with each other and were able to express the things that were bothering them.

When they both left for spring training in 1988, no one except those directly involved knew what had happened. And it never happened again. Since then father and son have had a very good relationship. Young Ken said he and his family decided to make the story public in 1992 in the hope it might prevent other teenagers from seeing suicide as a solution to their problems.

It took a great deal of courage for the Griffeys to break the story.

ON TO SEATTLE

Not knowing what had happened during the off-season, the Mariners sent Griffey, Jr., to San Bernadino. San Bernadino was a class A team in the California League. It was a step up from the Northwest League. But before going to San Bernadino, young Griffey spent a couple of weeks at the Mariners' spring training camp. It was a taste of the big leagues, and Junior liked it.

At San Bernadino, Junior began playing baseball like a superstar. It was amazing how he bounced back from the crisis of a few months earlier. He was playing loose and relaxed. Once again he was doing it all. He was hitting for average and for power. He was showing his great speed on the bases and in the outfield.

He became such a favorite of the fans that the team held a "Ken Griffey Poster Night," and the ballpark was sold out. Whenever young Griffey came up to the plate at home, the public announcer would ask, "What time is it?" And the fans would shout together, "Griffey Time!"

Once again, however, his daring in the outfield resulted in an injury. In a game on June 9, 1988, Griffey, Jr., tried to make a diving catch and injured his back. He was on the disabled list until August 15. But he had compiled such an outstanding record at San Bernadino that when he was ready to play again, the Mariners sent him to Vermont to play in the

Eastern League. He had moved up to double-A ball.

Before leaving San Bernadino, Griffey, Jr., batted .338 in 58 games. He had 13 doubles and 11 homers among his 74 hits. He also drove home 42 runs and stole 32 bases. He was leading the league in total bases and was second in average before he was hurt. Once again he was named the number-one major-league prospect in the league. There was no doubt that he had star quality written all over him.

It was already late in the season when young Griffey reached Vermont. Since he still had a sore back, he was a designated hitter for the final 17 games of the season. He hit .279 with a pair of homers and 10 runs batted in. Then in the Eastern League playoffs he got 8 hits in 18 at-bats for a .444 average with a club-best 7 RBIs. But as good as Junior

A daring outfielder right from his high school days, Junior made this spectacular catch in the Seattle Kingdome off a drive by the Rangers' Ruben Sierra in 1991.

had been, no one was ready for what would happen in 1989—the year would be a turning point for both Griffeys.

By 1989, Griffey, Sr., was back with his first team, the Cincinnati Reds. He had been signed by the Reds the year before, after playing the first part of the season with Atlanta. Unfortunately, Griffey, Sr., did not play well in 1988, finishing with a career low .255 batting average. Because he would be 40 years old at the beginning of 1989, he couldn't be sure if the Reds would keep him for another year or not.

Meanwhile, Griffey, Jr., was again invited to the Mariners' training camp in March 1989. The general opinion was that the 19-year-old player would probably be sent back to the minors for one full year at triple-A ball. The most likely stop was Calgary in the Pacific Coast League.

It didn't take long for the Mariners and their first-year manager, Jim Lefebvre, to notice how talented young Griffey was. When the exhibition games began, Manager Lefebvre made a quick decision: He would play Griffey, Jr., in center field every day.

"I want to take a good look at him," the manager said. "Then we'll see how it goes."

When reporters asked Griffey, Jr., about how it felt to be in a major-league camp, he replied, "Man, this is my twelfth spring training camp. That's ten with my dad and two on my own."

All those years hanging around the Cincinnati training camps taught him what to expect. But no one could hit for him. That he started doing on his own and didn't stop. At one point he had a 15-game hitting streak. It was the longest spring training hit streak in the Mariners' history. And as the pitchers got better, so did Griffey, Jr. During a three-week stretch in the spring he never went more than four at-bats without a hit.

He was also blazing on the field. In a game against the San Francisco Giants, he cut down the speedy Brett Butler, who was trying to go from first to third on a single. Young Griffey charged the ball and fired a strike to third. The ball never touched the ground.

Even with his success, Junior waited for the word to report to Calgary. When Manager Lefebvre called Griffey, Jr., to his office about a week before the season opened, young Griffey thought he was headed out. Instead he got a huge surprise.

"Congratulations," Lefebvre said. "You're my center fielder."

"When he said that, my heart started ticking again," said Griffey, Jr. "Those were probably the best words I've ever heard."

Lefebvre told the press that young Griffey was simply the best player for the position. "It's a good story," the manager said, "but I didn't bring him onto this ball club because he's a good story. He earned a spot here. He's outplayed a lot of people for that spot." It didn't hurt that the Mariners also needed a star player, someone the fans would want to come out and see.

Batting coach Gene Clines called young Griffey a natural. "You sit back and watch this kid, and he shows you what everybody is talking about. He can do it all."

Once it was announced that Griffey, Jr., had made the club, all eyes swung over to Cincinnati. There Manager Pete Rose decided to keep Griffey, Sr., on the ball club. He could still play, having hit .333 in his first

21 spring at-bats. Now father and son had a date with destiny. Once the 1989 season opened, they would become the first father-son pair to play in the majors at the same time.

STAR ROOKIE

Ken Griffey, Jr., had an amazing spring training. In 25 games he batted a sizzling .360. He also set Seattle spring records with 32 hits, 49 total bases, and 20 runs batted in. He had truly earned his spot. Young Griffey also loved the idea that his father was still in the big leagues. But he knew there would always be comparisons.

"It's harder being a baseball player when your father is a baseball player," he said. "People will say, 'Your dad hit .300 lifetime, so you have to hit .310 to

It was a happy day for both Griffey, Sr., (left) and Griffey, Jr., in 1989 when they became the first father and son to play in the majors at the same time.

be better.' They put you in a category with your father, and that's not fair because you are two different people."

Griffey, Jr., quickly showed he was his own person. The Mariners opened the season against the powerful Oakland Athletics and their ace pitcher Dave Stewart. Young Griffey's first major league at-bat came in the first inning. He took Stewart's first pitch, then stroked a fastball off the base of the right-field wall at the Oakland Coliseum for a solid double. Not a bad way to start a career.

When the Mariners returned to the Kingdome in Seattle, Griffey, Jr., gave the hometown fans a treat. In his first home at-bat, his first swing resulted in a long, opposite-field home run to left field. The fans gave him a standing ovation. They had already taken this 19-year-old phenomenon to heart.

By May 12, Junior was hitting a surprising .303 with 3 homers and 9 RBIs. He was definitely one of the best rookies in the league. At the same time, Griffey, Sr., was playing a utility role in Cincinnati. He was a part-time player and pinch hitter, batting just .227. But he was thrilled to be in the big leagues at the same time as his son. He knew that Junior was going to be the big story from now on.

At the All-Star break Junior was hitting a solid .279. He now had 13 homers, second on the team to Jeffrey Leonard's 15. He had also driven in 38 runs, third best on the ball club. His 10 steals were second to Harold Reynolds's on the Mariners, and he continued to play outstanding defense with just 3 errors in his first 81 games. Better yet, the Mariners were still around the .500 mark and had a chance for their first winning year ever.

Although Griffey, Jr., didn't make the 1989 American League All-Star Team, he still received 79,051 write-in votes. That was more write-ins than for anyone else who wasn't on the official All-Star ballot. It looked as if he were on the way to becoming Rookie of the Year. But a freak accident on July 25 changed everything.

Griffey, Jr.'s, first at-bat in the major leagues came on April 3, 1989. The result was a ringing double off the Oakland A's Dave Stewart, then one of the top pitchers in the American League.

Griffey, Jr., was stepping out of the shower in his hotel room in Chicago when he slipped. He quickly threw out his right hand to keep himself from falling. The impact fractured a bone that ran from his wrist to his little finger. He was placed on the disabled list and would be out nearly a month. At the time, Griffey, Jr., had his average up to .287 with 13 homers and 45 RBIs.

The Mariners had dropped under .500 and were beset by a number of injuries, but Griffey's injury caused the team to suffer. "It's going to have an effect on a lot of things, team-wise and Rookie of the Year-wise," said Manager Lefebvre.

Griffey, Jr., returned to the lineup August 20, but the month on the shelf had taken a toll. Junior hit just .181 in September and October. He finished the year in a slump, but his numbers were still impressive for one so young. He wound up with a .264 batting average in 127 games. He also had 23 doubles, 16 home runs, and 61 runs batted in. He had those numbers despite missing 35 games.

"He was trying to catch up with the other Rookie of the Year candidates with one swing," said Manager Lefebvre. "It wasn't surprising for a 19-year-old kid, really. He just lost his poise."

Griffey admitted that his manager was right. "I was worrying about hitting the ball 700 feet," he said. "I just wanted 20 home runs."

It was another losing season for the Mariners, but in the eyes of nearly everyone, the team finally had a potential star: the kid they were calling Junior.

A HAPPY REUNION

Junior wasn't the only one in the family to turn in an overall solid season in 1989. Like his son, Griffey, Sr., had his ups and downs, but rebounded from a slow start to fill an important role for the Reds. He wound up with a .263 batting average in 106 games. He also hit eight homers and drove home 30 runs. It wasn't like the old days, but certainly not bad for a 40-year-old ballplayer. In fact, it was enough to convince Griffey, Sr., to return for the 1990 season.

It was Junior, however, who was making the news early in the new year. He was hot all spring and continued to swing a scorching bat the first month of the season. At one point in the early going he was leading the league in hitting with a .395 average. He was also near the top in hits, total bases, home runs, and RBIs. At age 20 he was still the youngest player in the majors.

"He's still a big kid," said hitting coach Gene Clines. "When he finally buckles down and gets serious about the game, there's no telling what kind of numbers he will put on the board. I don't think anybody's ever been that good at that age. He's just a natural."

Junior certainly was playing the game like a natural. He didn't worry about who was pitching or what kinds of pitches he threw. He just got up there and hit. In the field, he was just as good. In a game at Yankee Stadium in New York, he showed everyone what he could do.

The Yankees' Jesse Barfield hit a deep drive to left center field. Griffey took off at the crack of the bat and raced toward the wall in left center. He hit the warning track at full speed, then took two giant steps, planted one

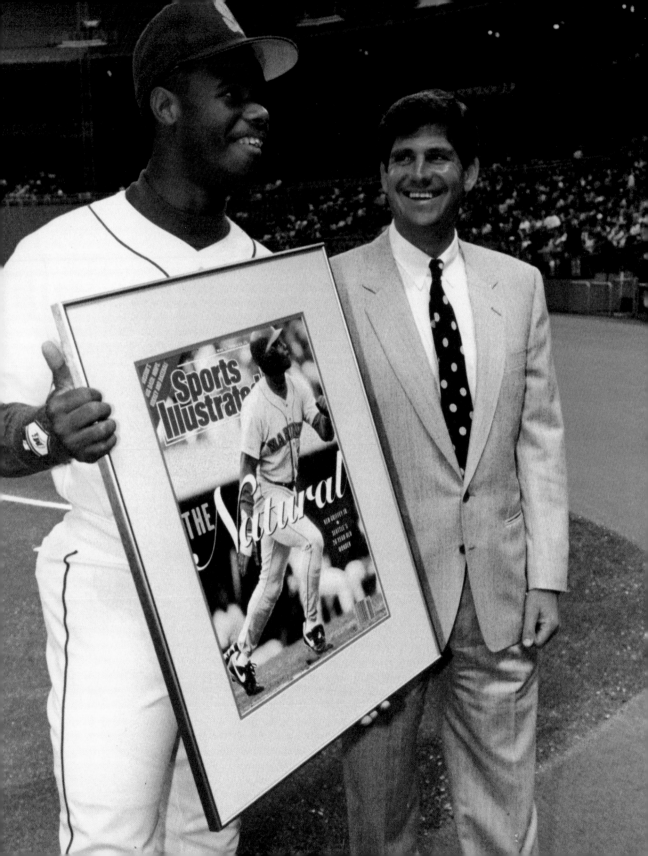

cleat halfway up the foam padding on the wall, and leaped. His right arm cleared the 8-foot (2.44-meter) high wall with room to spare. For a second it disappeared over the wall. But when he pulled it back, the ball was in his glove. It was an amazing catch. Junior called it his best ever.

"As I jumped, I thought I had a chance," he said later. "That's the first one I've caught going over the wall, in practice or a game."

But it wouldn't be the only one. In the same series with the Yankees he made a diving backhand catch of a ball in the gap to help the Mariners hold a lead. He also made a brilliant catch against the Athletics' Rickey Henderson in Oakland in mid-April. Griffey, Jr., raced straight back to center and took the drive over-the-shoulder with his back to home plate. The bases were loaded at the time, so he saved three or four runs.

"Every time he makes one of those plays, you think he'll never top it," said Manager Lefebvre. "You can't believe how much it picks up the entire club. He's going to be one of the real marquee players in this league. That's one thing his father, as great as he was, never was."

In a sense, that was true. Griffey, Sr., had been a very fine ball player in his prime. Griffey, Jr., however, had the skills to be an all-time great. Although he had been injured several times in the minors trying to make circus catches, he still climbed walls and dove for balls in the big leagues. Getting injured just wasn't part of his game plan.

In May 1990, Seattle Mariners' principal owner,
Jeff Smulyan, presented Griffey, Jr., with a blowup
of a Sports Illustrated *cover that featured the*
rookie as "The Natural."

Junior continued to have a great first half of the 1990 season. By the All-Star break he was hitting .331 with 12 homers and 40 runs batted in. His batting average was second in the American League to Rickey Henderson's .335. Young Griffey was leading the league with 107 hits. Not surprisingly, he was voted the starting center fielder on the American League All-Star team. It was quite an honor for a 20-year-old.

By mid-August, Griffey, Jr., was hitting .323 with 16 homers and 56 RBIs. He was putting together an almost superstar season. He trailed only Henderson in the batting race and continued to play outstanding ball in center field. The Mariners were once again a .500 team, and were becoming better players.

Things weren't going nearly so well for Griffey, Sr. He was seeing very little action with the Reds, hitting just .210 in 45 games. Being used mainly as a pinch hitter, he had just 62 at-bats, 1 homer, and 8 RBIs. The Reds were favoring their younger players. There was simply no room for a 40-year-old part-time player.

On August 18, the Reds asked Griffey, Sr., to go on the disabled list. They wanted an open space on their roster for a younger player. Griffey refused, saying he wasn't injured. Instead, the Reds placed him on waivers. That meant any club could claim him. The Mariners took him, and it made headlines all over the country. Now father and son would get to play pro ball together.

Many felt the Mariners signed Griffey, Sr., as a publicity stunt, a way to bring in more fans. Manager Lefebvre denied this. "He [Griffey, Sr.] is not here so we can say we were the first to have a father and son on the team," he said. "He's here to make a contribution on the field and in the clubhouse."

Griffey, Sr.'s, signing set up the game on August 31 when father and son played together for the first time. Griffey, Sr., said it was the best thing that ever happened to him, while Ken, Jr., said it was like playing catch with his dad in the backyard.

JUNIOR ON HIS OWN

The first week after Griffey, Sr., joined the Mariners, he proved his worth. Not only did the Mariners win four of five games, but Junior's father was playing very well. After five games he had a batting average of .421, getting 8 hits in 19 at-bats, and driving home 5 runs. In one game he had three hits.

"There was never a doubt in my mind that I could still do the job," Griffey, Sr., said. "I usually wasn't in the lineup long enough with the Reds to get three hits."

Oddly enough, Junior slumped a bit after his father joined the team. When the 1990 season ended, young Griffey was hitting an even .300. He also finished with 22 homers and 80 runs batted in, as well as 16 bases stolen. Overall, it was an outstanding season for a 20-year-old player.

Griffey, Sr., played in 21 games for the Mariners and wound up hitting .377, adding 3 homers and 18 RBIs. Playing alongside his son had given him a new lease on his baseball life. He decided to come back for another season in 1991. That made his son happy, too.

*Junior is all smiles as he brings his father's hat to him after
the senior Griffey lost it while making a running catch.*

Now if they could only make the team a winner. Seattle finished the
year at 77-85 and in fifth place. They had three promising young pitchers
in Erik Hanson, Brian Holman, and Randy Johnson. Edgar Martinez, Alvin
Davis, Harold Reynolds, and Jeffrey Leonard could do damage with the
bat. The team seemed to be getting better.

Then in March, after the start of spring training, Griffey, Sr., was in an
auto accident. He suffered neck and back injuries, which put his future in

doubt. "If I can't help [the team], I won't put the decision on the team," he said. "I'll make it, and I'll make the right one."

Griffey, Sr., opened the season on the disabled list, and the team lost its first six games. Griffey, Jr., was the only bright spot, once again off to a hot start with the bat. The team soon began playing better. Griffey, Sr., came off the disabled list and was hitting well once again. After the first month the team was 12-13. Junior was hitting .319, and Griffey, Sr., was hitting .308.

Toward the end of May, Junior had the worst slump of his career. He was hitless in 18 straight at-bats but didn't press. His average fell from .343 to .292 before he snapped out of it with a three-hit game against the Yankees. At last the club was winning. On May 26 they were 23-20.

By mid-June Junior was hitting .291, and Senior was back on the disabled list with a sore neck. It was soon learned that his problem was a ruptured disk. Word was he would be out until at least July. At his age this kind of injury might end a career.

At mid-season Junior was again a starter on the All-Star team. He had two hits as the American League won 4-2. At the break he was hitting just .281, with 9 homers and 38 RBIs. He was cheered by news that his father still hoped to play again. Griffey, Sr., wanted to try it before the season ended. The team was at 43-43, just six and a half games behind division-leading Minnesota. After the break Junior began hitting well. He had his average up over the .300 mark and began driving in more runs. Once again, he was one of the most feared hitters in the league. By the end of August he was at .328, fifth in the batting race. He was third in doubles with 35, had 17 homers and 72 RBIs. He was putting together a great season.

Junior had hit .410 in July and .377 in August. There really wasn't a hotter hitter in baseball. Manager Lefebvre thought he was as valuable as any player in the league.

"For what he's done for this club he definitely deserves MVP consideration," said Lefebvre. "He's hitting well over .300, and if you could attach an average to his defense, he'd be hitting about .800."

The Mariners finished the season with their first winning record ever, 83-79. And Ken Griffey, Jr., finished with his best year ever. He wound up with a .327 batting average, hit 22 homers, and drove home 100 runs. He also had 42 doubles and 18 stolen bases. Defensively, he made his usual great catches and had just four errors in the outfield. At age 21 he had superstar numbers.

Shortly after the 1991 season ended, there was some sad news. Griffey, Sr., announced his retirement. He had stopped playing in September when he had surgery to repair the disk in his neck that was injured in the auto accident. At age 41, he thought it would be too tough to come back for another season. He retired with a .296 lifetime batting average for 19 seasons—a very good career.

Now the spotlight was firmly on the younger Griffey. In December he was awarded his second straight Gold Glove, given to the top defensive player at each position. This time he also received the Silver Bat Award as the top offensive player at his position. Griffey, Jr., and shortstop Cal Ripken, Jr., of Baltimore, were the only American Leaguers to win both awards that year.

In the eyes of most, Ken Griffey, Jr., could only get better. His batting average has gone from .264 to .300 to .327 in his first three seasons. No other player in baseball history has increased his average by 25 points or more in each of his first three years. He has performed brilliantly and has helped to turn the Mariners into a winning team.

Ken Griffey, Jr., has always credited his father for much of his success. They have survived a personal crisis to form a close and loving relationship. Barring injury, young Griffey could become one of baseball's brightest stars of the 1990s. If he plays as long as his father did, there will have been a Griffey starring in the majors for nearly 40 consecutive years.

Griffey, Jr., jokes with the A's Harold Baines (left) and the Giants' Will Clark (right) during a practice session at the SkyDome in Toronto.

THE GRIFFEYS: HIGHLIGHTS

1950	Ken Griffey, Sr., born on April 10 in Donora, Pennsylvania.
1969	Ken Griffey, Sr., picked by Cincinnati Reds on 29th round of draft. Ken Griffey, Jr., born on November 21 in Donora, Pennsylvania.
1973	Ken Griffey, Sr.'s, first year in the major league.
1975	Ken Griffey, Sr., becomes Reds' regular right fielder and has a .305 batting average. Reds win the World Series and become known as the "Big Red Machine."
1976	Ken Griffey, Sr., bats .336 and steals 34 bases. Reds win the World Series.
1980	Ken Griffey, Sr., named Most Valuable Player of the All-Star Game.
1986	Ken Griffey, Jr., leads his team to the Connie Mack League World Series.
1987	Ken Griffey, Jr., the nation's number one draft choice, picked by Seattle Mariners on June 2, begins professional career in the Northwest league. Ken Griffey, Jr., named to the all-league team, and voted top major-league prospect in the Northwest League by *Baseball America*.
1988	Ken Griffey, Jr., plays for San Bernadino. Finishes the season playing double-A ball in the Eastern League in Vermont. Ken Griffey, Sr., returns to the Cincinnati Reds.
1989	Ken Griffey, Jr., makes the Seattle Mariners at age 19. The two Griffeys become the first father-son pair to play in the majors at the same time.
1990	Ken Griffey, Sr., signed by the Seattle Mariners. The Griffeys play together on August 31. Ken Griffey, Jr., voted starter on the American League All-Star Team. Ken Griffey, Jr., receives Gold Glove award.
1991	Ken Griffey, Sr., retires from baseball. Ken Griffey, Jr., named to All-Star Team for the second consecutive year. Ken Griffey, Jr., receives Gold Glove and Silver Bat Awards.
1992	Ken Griffey, Jr., named Most Valuable Player of the All-Star Game.

FIND OUT MORE

Duden, Jane. *Baseball*. New York: Macmillan, 1991.

Gutman, Bill. *Baseball's Hot New Stars*. New York: Pocket Books, 1989.

Kaplan, Rick. *The Official Baseball Hall of Fame Book of Super Stars*. New York: Simon & Schuster, 1989.

Sally, Dick and Tom Dipace. *Home Run Kings*. New York: Simon & Schuster, 1989.

Monteleone, John. *A Day in the Life of a Major League Baseball Player*. Mahwah, N.J.: Troll, 1992.

Murphy, Jim. *Baseball's All-Time All-Stars*. Boston: Houghton Mifflin, 1984.

How to write to Ken Griffey, Jr.:

Ken Griffey, Jr.
c/o Seattle Mariners
P.O. Box 4100
Seattle, Washington 98104

INDEX

All-Star break, 32, 38
All-Star Game, 1980, 14
All-Star Game, 1990, 38
All-Star Game, 1991, 41
American League, 33, 38, 41
Atlanta, Georgia, 18
Atlanta Braves, 15, 28

Baines, Harold, 43
Baltimore Orioles, 42
Barfield, Jesse, 35
Baseball America, 24
Bellingham, Washington, 21, 22, 24
Bench, Johnny, 9
Big Red Machine, 5, 9, 14
Boston Red Sox, 10
Butler, Brett, 29

Calgary, Canada, 28, 29
California League, 25
Cameron, Mike, 19
Canada, 22
Chicago, Illinois, 34
Cincinnati, Ohio, 13, 15, 16, 17
Cincinnati Reds, 5, 6, 9, 13, 14, 28, 29,
    32, 35, 38
Clark, Will, 43
Clines, Gene, 29, 35
Concepcion, Dave, 9
Connie Mack League, 17
Connie Mack World Series, 17

Davis, Alvin, 40
DiMaggio, Joe, 15
Disabled list, 26, 34, 38, 41

Donora High School, 7, 9
Donora, Pennsylvania, 7
Draft, 9, 21
Drago, Dick, 10

Eastern League, 27

Fisk, Carlton, 10
Foster, George, 9

Gehrig, Lou, 15
Geronimo, Cesar, 9
Gold Glove, 42
Griffey, Alberta, 9, 10, 13, 16, 17
Griffey, Buddy, 7, 9
Griffey, Craig, 10, 13
Griffey, Ken, Jr.
    batting average, 24, 27, 31, 32, 34, 38,
        39, 41, 42
    birth of, 10
    in Connie Mack League, 17
    football and, 17, 18
    injuries, 24, 26
    in Little League, 10
    racism and, 23, 24
    RBIs, 24, 27, 31, 34, 38, 39
    suicide attempt, 25
Griffey, Ken, Sr.
    bases stolen, 10
    batting average, 9, 10, 15, 28, 29, 32, 35,
        38, 39, 41, 42
    birth of, 7
    in minor leagues, 9
    sports and, 9

Griffey, Ruth, 9

Hall of Fame, 17
Hanson, Erik, 40
Henderson, Rickey, 37, 38
Holman, Brian, 40

Instructional League, 24

Jackson, Bo, 5, 6-7
Johnson, Randy, 40

Kansas City Royals, 5
Kuhn, Bowie, 15

Lefebvre, Jim, 28, 29, 34, 37, 38, 42
Leonard, Jeffrey, 40
Little League, 14, 17
Little Red Machine, 14

Mack, Connie, 17
Mantle, Mickey, 15
Martinez, Edgar, 40
May, Lee, 14
McRae, Brian, 14
Minnesota Twins, 41
Moeller High School, 17-19, 21
  football at, 17
Morgan, Joe, 9
Mount Airy, Ohio, 14, 25
Most Valuable Player, 14, 15, 42
Musial, Stan "The Man," 7

National League, 15
New York City, 10, 18
New York Yankees, 15, 35, 37
Northwest League, 21, 23, 24, 26

Oakland Athletics, 32, 37, 43
Oakland Coliseum, 32

Pacific Coast League, 28
Puerto Rico, 13
Perez, Eduardo, 14
Perez, Tony, 9, 14
Perez, Victor, 14
Philadelphia Athletics, 17
Player of the Week, 23
Player of the Year, 19
Providence Hospital, 25

Reynolds, Harold, 6, 40
Ripken, Cal, Jr., 42
Riverfront Stadium, 13
Rose, Pete, 9, 29
Rose, Pete, Jr., 14
Ruth, Babe, 15

San Bernardino, California, 26-27
San Francisco Giants, 29, 43
Seattle, Washington, 21
Seattle Kingdome, 5, 27, 32
Seattle Mariners, 5, 7, 21, 26, 28, 29, 32,
  34, 37, 38, 39, 42, 43
Sierra, Ruben, 27
Silver Bat Award, 42
Smulyan, Jeff, 37
Sports Illustrated, 37
Stewart, Dave, 32, 33
Sweet, Rick, 23

Toronto SkyDome, 43

Watson, Bob, 16
World Series, 6, 9, 10

Yankee Stadium, 35